make your own . . .
Scotch Whisky

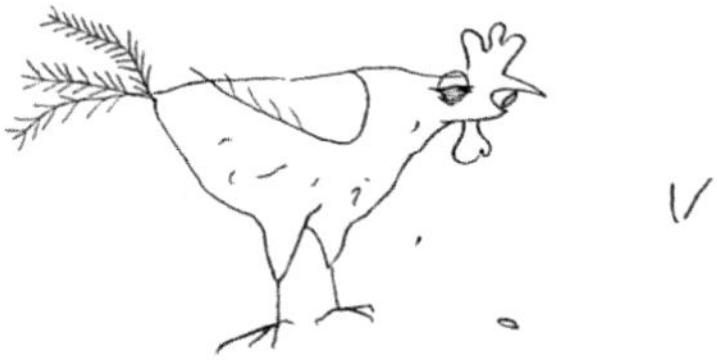

make your own . . .
Scotch Whisky

original text

Adam Bergius

(former Chairman & Export Director
of Wm. Teacher & Sons)

original illustration

Rowland Emett

© Allied Distillers

First published 1972
This edition 1995
Argyll Publishing
Glendaruel
Argyll PA22 3AE
Scotland

British Library Cataloguing-in-Publication Data.
A catalogue record for this book is available from the British Library.

ISBN 1 874640 96 3

Origination
Cordfall Ltd, Glasgow

Printing
BPC Paulton Books Limited

To Adam Bergius
whose wit and inspiration
have given us this gem.

Foreword

A sense of humour is one of the most precious gifts
known to man. Combined with an allegorical tale,
it makes for a story that holds up in the memory
and is fun to explore over and over again. Such was
the achievement and originality of the creators of
make your own Scotch Whisky.

Over thirty years ago, imagination combined
with a bold instinct for fun to bring two great men
together. So it was when Rowland Emett, artist and
inventor joined Adam Bergius, proprietor and
export director of Teacher's Scotch Whisky, to
create the original make your own Scotch booklet.

Adam wrote the text to fill in a long flight
home from Australia. As a master of the
understatement, the author unfolds the magic of

the process in crafting Scotch malt whisky by referring to things that touch our everyday Scottish lives. Combine this with Emett's inventive depictions and you have imagery of the Scotch production process that is inimitable, sets the imagination alight, and the lips smiling.

Read on and take the time to enjoy yourself.

Bill Bergius
great, great grandson of
William Teacher,
Founder of
Teacher's Highland Cream

Scotch Whisky

First pipe in a suitable
supply of Scottish hill water, and add to this a
goodly quantity of barley, allowing it to soak for 48
hours.

Then strain off the water, and lay out the wet
barley on a cool floor in a great heap. It will start to
grow, and in doing so, will become hot.

So make a wooden spade, and every few hours turn it over, each time spreading it a little thinner on the floor to keep it cool. As barley grows twenty four hours a day, you will have to set an alarm and get up regularly to carry out turning throughout the night.

This process takes only
eleven days, and in your spare time you will have
been able to construct a fireplace at the foot of a

small brick tower which should have a wire gauze floor half-way up and a wooden imitation of a Chinese pagoda at the top with a hole in the roof.

Take your eleven-day-old barley, which by this time will have grown a little shoot and a root, and spread it out carefully on the wire floor. What you have made is called malt. In the fireplace you must now build a huge fire of peat.

This is a type of decomposed Scottish vegetation which is dug out of a bog the previous Spring, and carefully dried in what sunshine the following Scottish summer has to offer. This fuel is important as the peat smoke, which has a most nostalgic and haunting aroma, imparts some of this to the drying malt, and ultimately to the finished whisky, giving it flavour and character in much the same way as the smoke of wood chips gives us the delectable and appetising flavour of well-cured bacon or kippered herrings.

Every three hours dig over the drying malt, as otherwise it will burn on the lower side.

Unfortunately, as the fire cannot be put out, you will find the working conditions far from agreeable, and you will also notice that the smoke is not particularly nostalgic, but extremely haunting, and it will most probably haunt your clothes for the next four or five days.

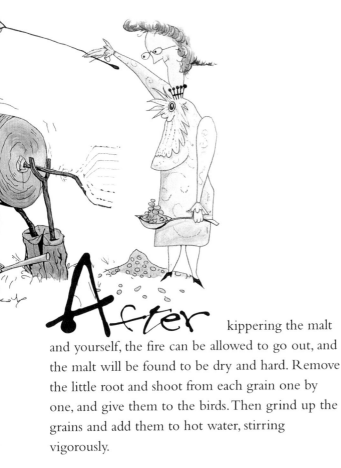

After kippering the malt and yourself, the fire can be allowed to go out, and the malt will be found to be dry and hard. Remove the little root and shoot from each grain one by one, and give them to the birds. Then grind up the grains and add them to hot water, stirring vigorously.

Drain off the liquid, allowing it to cool in a separate vessel and add some yeast (you can get this from the baker). Bubbles will soon appear and the sugar in the malt you have made will gradually be eaten by the yeast and turned into weak alcohol. Leave this to go on for three days, but do not taste it as it is horrible, and is called Wash.

Scotch Whisky

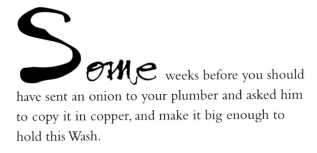

Some weeks before you should
have sent an onion to your plumber and asked him
to copy it in copper, and make it big enough to
hold this Wash.

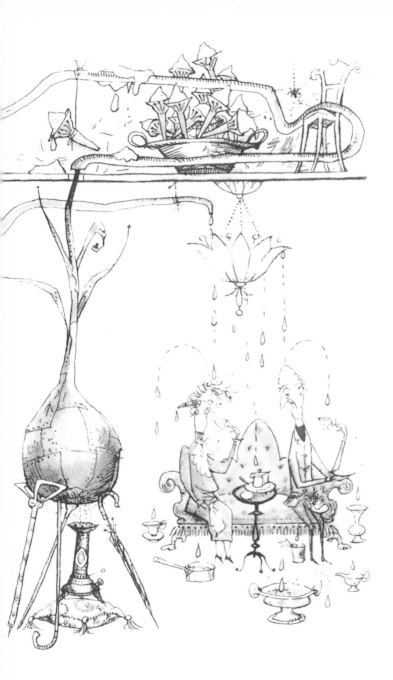

Now you must fill it up and connect up the end of the onion with a corkscrew-shaped pipe which should be kept immersed in running water.

Put a Primus stove underneath and wait for the drips at the end of the pipe.

When these stop, empty out the Still and clean it carefully, putting the product of the last distillation back in again. You then have to do the same thing all over again.

You won't recognise what you have made, but if you are in Scotland, and if you put it in a oak cask and keep it there for three years, then you are legally allowed to call it Scotch Whisky.

However, as you have
made it outside the law, you will not be allowed to
call it anything, and, in fact, you had better keep
very quiet about it.

If you live elsewhere, you will just have made
whisky. It may be good, or it may be bad, for no-
one knows what the product of a new distillery will
be like until it has been made, matured and tasted,
and the different shapes of Stills make different
kinds of whisky.

Unfortunately, if you want to make something like the great brands of Scotch, you must also produce a Scotch Grain Whisky to blend with your malt whisky, and, of course, keep all your whiskies very much longer than the minimum legal three years.

Grain whisky is a type of whisky which has none of the strong robust character of the malt whiskies. It is rather thin in body and has only a very little flavour, but it is mild and flowery to the nose. It is made largely by magic in large distilleries, and simply does not work on a small scale.

Your family or neighbours would undoubtedly object if you converted your whole house into a distillery, so this problem can be dismissed from your mind.

So there it is, after all this trouble you cannot even, after waiting for years and years, make a whisky to equal the great brands of Scotch.

The experienced blender is as the experienced host, and the finished blend is as the successful party. Invite the mediocre and your party will be mediocre. Skilfully blend people of strong character and your party will scintillate. Whiskies of character and personality are invited to make the great brands of Scotch.

We would hate to dissuade you from "Do It Yourself", but with the industry having over 150 years of experience of whisky and blending, and every blend tasted by an expert blender, we feel we can perform a useful service for you, and bring to you something you will enjoy and cherish.

When Government taxes on whisky are deducted, it is really very inexpensive, and even if you do try to make it yourself, the Excise will surely find you out. The fines are very heavy, and the prisons alas unlicensed.

William Teacher, creator of Teacher's Highland
Cream, set up in business in Glasgow in the wine
and spirit trade in 1830, with emphasis from the
beginning on Scotch Whisky. All blended Scotch is
made from two kinds of whisky – malt and grain –
but Teacher's Highland Cream has an exceptionally
high malt content – at least 45%, a feature which
contributes to Teacher's unique character and
flavour and to the consumption of Teacher's in
almost every country around the world today.